To Mom + Dad,

Read before your fireplace blazing — to all the children eyes amazing.

Love,
Christelle

Christmas 2021

To my friend Lisa,

This was Joe's mom's book, but we couldn't think of anyone who would enjoy this like you!

Merry Christmas!

love,
Joe + Terry

TEXAS NIGHT
BEFORE CHRISTMAS

TEXAS NIGHT BEFORE CHRISTMAS

Written and Illustrated by JAMES RICE

PELICAN PUBLISHING COMPANY

GRETNA 1988

First printing, September 1986
Second printing, October 1988

Library of Congress Cataloging-in-Publication Data

Rice, James, 1934–
    Texas night before Christmas.

    Summary: With a team of recalcitrant longhorns
pulling his sleigh, "Santy" pays a visit to a family
on the Texas prairie, bringing gifts and Christmas
cheer.
    [1. Santa Claus—Fiction.   2. Christmas—Fiction.
3. Frontier and pioneer life—Fiction.   4. Texas—
Fiction.   5. Stories in rhyme]   I. Title.
PZ8.3.R36Te   1986   [Fic]   86-9445
ISBN 0-88289-603-2

Printed in the United States of America

Published by Pelican Publishing Company, Inc.
1101 Monroe Street, Gretna, Louisiana 70053

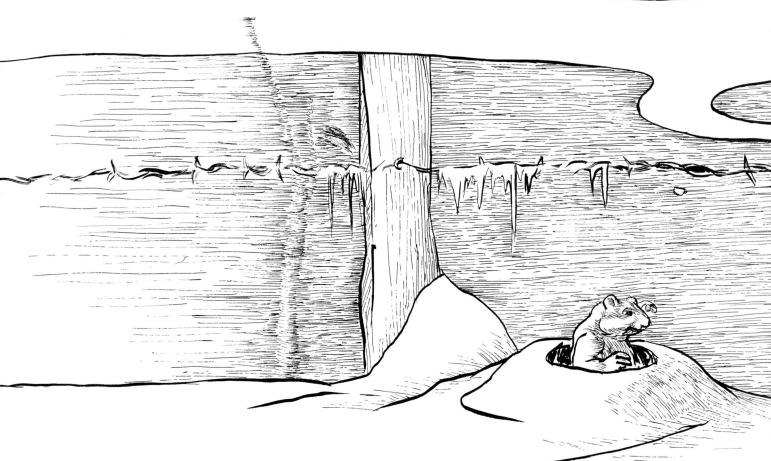

'Twas the night before Christmas
in the cold wintry fog.
Nary a critter was movin',
nor a lone prairie dog.

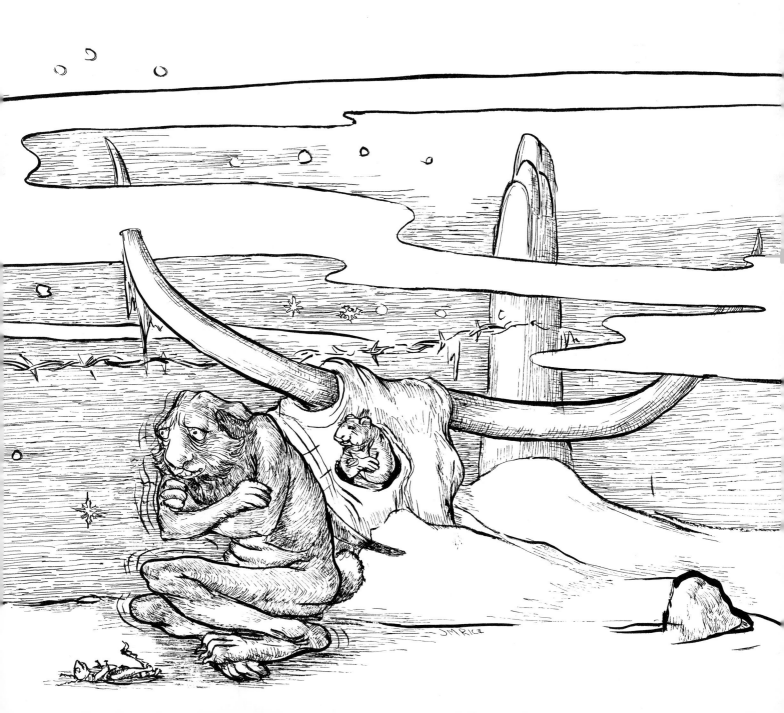

Then from out of the north
    the breeze gave a stir;
An icy cold blast
    swirled the fog in a blur.

A blue Texas norther
    roared over the plains.
The cold fairly whistled
    through the loose winderpanes.

I poked at the farplace
to stir up a flame—
The embers glowed redder,
but the cold stayed the same.

Ma fixed up our dinner
　　to be ready next day
And thought about Christmas
　　a few hours away.

Our scuffed boots were assembled
　　on the floor pair by pair
Where Santy would find 'em,
　　for he soon would be there.

The younguns were bundled
   down snug in their covers,
A sprout of a girl
   and her two older brothers.

So me in my long johns
   and Ma in her gown
Warmed up by the far
   'fore we laid ourselves down.

Then from out on the range
   there came such a ruckus,
I ran to the winder
   to see what the fuss was.

Through the blue winter blizzard
   a scene came to sight;
I squinted to see,
   for there waren't much light.

JM RICE

There stompin' and snortin'
and pawin' the ground
Were eight scroungy longhorns
stampedin' around

In front of a wagon
piled full as could be
With boxes and bundles
as high as a tree.

Then a bellerin' yell
   soon set them all straight
From a fat li'l ole ramrod
   who put fear in the eight.

Well, they waren't really scairt—
   no harm would he cause—
For their longhorn head honcho
   was old Santy Claus!

He got their attention
 and called them by name,
"Hey, Leadfoot and Waleye—
 git up there, Culhane!

"Come on, Gimp and Flopear
 and Scarface—start draggin',
Git on, Sam and High-Hips,
 let's move this here wagon!"

Old Leadfoot, he bellered
and lifted his head,
Then straight on they trampled
through Ma's flower bed.

They laid the gate flat,
    and the clothesline went, too.
Nothin' stood in their way
    as they flat-footed through.

Santy pulled them up short
    on top of the roof
After wrecking the porch
    with them clodhopper hoofs.

They rocked our sod shanty,
    the dirt sifted down,
And then through the chimney
    Santy came with a bound!

He was dressed all in rawhide
    with a Stetson on top.
His big Texas boots
    hit the floor with a clop.

He shook his great belly
    and stomped with each foot,
Which knocked off a shower
    of mud, ash, and soot.

His eyes were both squinty
    and his skin was like leather
From too much exposure
    to the raw Texas weather.

He looked tough as a horseshoe,
    but I felt no alarm,
'Cause a wink of his eye
    showed he'd do us no harm.

A feed bag of toys
    he flung from his back,
And with nary a word
    he opened the sack.

He filled all the boots
and piled them up high,
Then looked out the winder
and up at the sky.

The cold Texas norther
   still whistled and blew,
But more younguns was waitin'—
   his work wasn't through.

It was hard to just leave
   and walk through the door
To face all them longhorns
   and the cold as before.

He drank some hot mud
   and hunched close to the heat
To soak up the warmth
   and thaw his cold feet.

He could no longer dally
   or put off the chore,
So he gave us a wink
   and pushed through the door.

He prodded the longhorns
to get on the go,
And the wagon took off
through the fog and the snow.

He called over the norther
    'fore he went out of sight,
"Merry Christmas, y'heah?
    and y'all have a good night!"